If You Were a BEAR

IF YOU WERE A
BEAR

by Rachel Mazur
Illustrated by Sarina Jepsen

Sequoia Natural History Association • Three Rivers, CA

Rachel and Sarina would like to thank Jaybo, Pete, Julie, Rick, Areta, and the 3R writing group for their helpful suggestions and encouragement during the preparation of this book.

Text copyright © 2008 Rachel Mazur
Illustrations copyright © 2008 Sarina Jepsen
Design and layout by Julie Mazur Tribe

ISBN: 978-1-878441-29-4
Library of Congress Control Number: 2007941612

Published by the Sequoia Natural History Association
47050 Generals Highway #10, Three Rivers, CA 93271
www.sequoiahistory.org

Printed in the United States on recycled paper
Second printing, July 2009

The Sequoia Natural History Association is a nonprofit education partner of the National Park Service at Sequoia and Kings Canyon National Parks and Devils Postpile National Monument, providing programs, membership benefits, books and interpretive products, and funding for education and natural resource projects. For more children's books on nature and national parks, visit our online bookstore at www.sequoiahistory.org.

For Henry, LB, and the gang -R.M.
For Gavin, with love -S.J.

Imagine that you fell asleep,
a person tucked in bed.
But woke up in the morning
as a black bear cub instead!

What would you eat? Where would you sleep?
How would you spend your day?
How long would your claws be?
How much would you weigh?

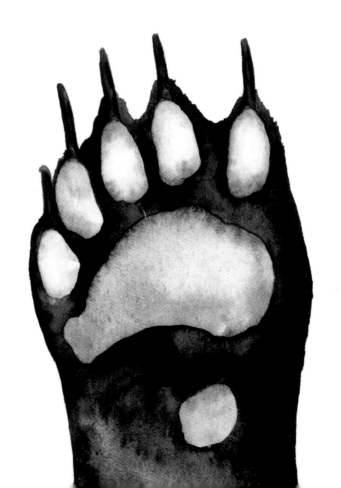

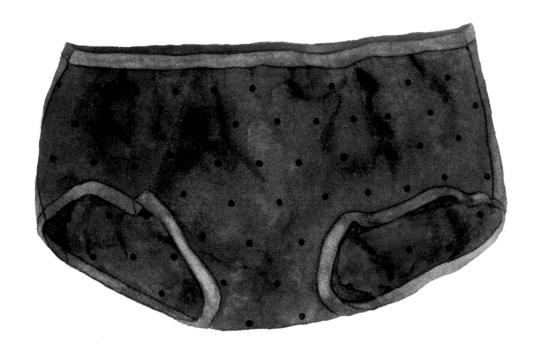

Would you wear shoes? A shirt? A hat?
Or purple underwear?
How would your days be different
if you became a bear?

You'd start your life in winter,
snuggled deep inside a den.
Born smaller than a football,
with a sibling for a friend.

Inside the den, you'd drink mom's milk
to quickly grow in size.
You'd soon have fur, strong teeth and
claws, and open up your eyes.

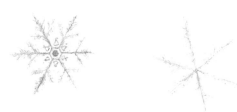

You'd find your fur might not be black—
it could be blonde or brown.
You'd test your little padded paws
to softly move around.

Then once the days got warmer
and your mom was in the mood,
she'd lead the family from the den
and start to look for food.

In springtime you would eat new grass
and roots and tasty plants.
In summer you might eat your fill
of berries, fish, and ants.

Some days you'd look for honey,
probing beehives with your tongue.
Something so sweet must be a treat,
'cause likely you'd get stung!

With teeth and claws you'd tear up logs
to find the ants inside.
And as they run, you'd use your tongue
to eat them 'fore they hide.

Your sense of smell would serve you well
to find delicious meats.
Your sense of sight would guide you right
to other tasty treats.

And when you were not eating,
you'd have lots of time to play.
To climb and run, to just have fun...

or nap the day away.

Your days would have adventure
and you'd safely wander free.
But when your mom would sound alarm
you'd scramble up a tree.

And as you grew, you'd learn to tell
the safe things from the dangers.
You'd stand up tall and sniff the air
to learn of coming strangers.

When autumn came you'd spend your days
up climbing in the trees,
and eating crunchy acorns
'til the ground began to freeze.

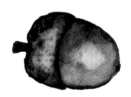

Your mom would then prepare a den
as snow

began

to

fall.

You'd snuggle in to sleep for months
and would not eat at all!

This is the way things rightly go
when bears are wild and free.
But things go wrong when food's left out
by folks like you and me.

Now food can mean an ice cream cone
or seed meant for the birds,
Or scraps of meat left on a grill,
or garbage by the curb.

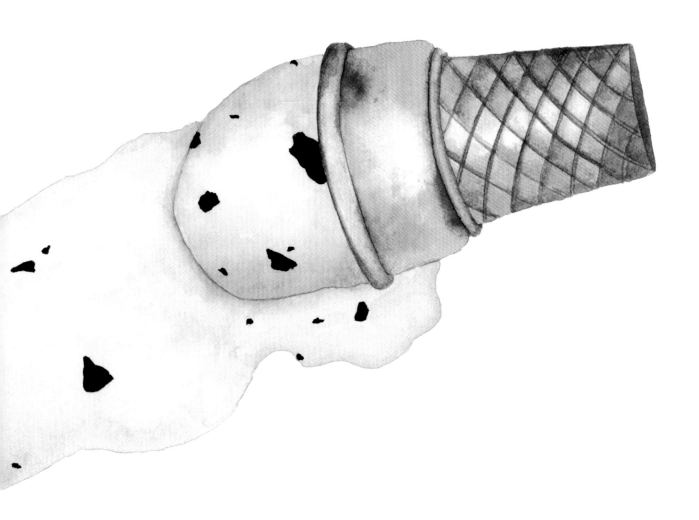

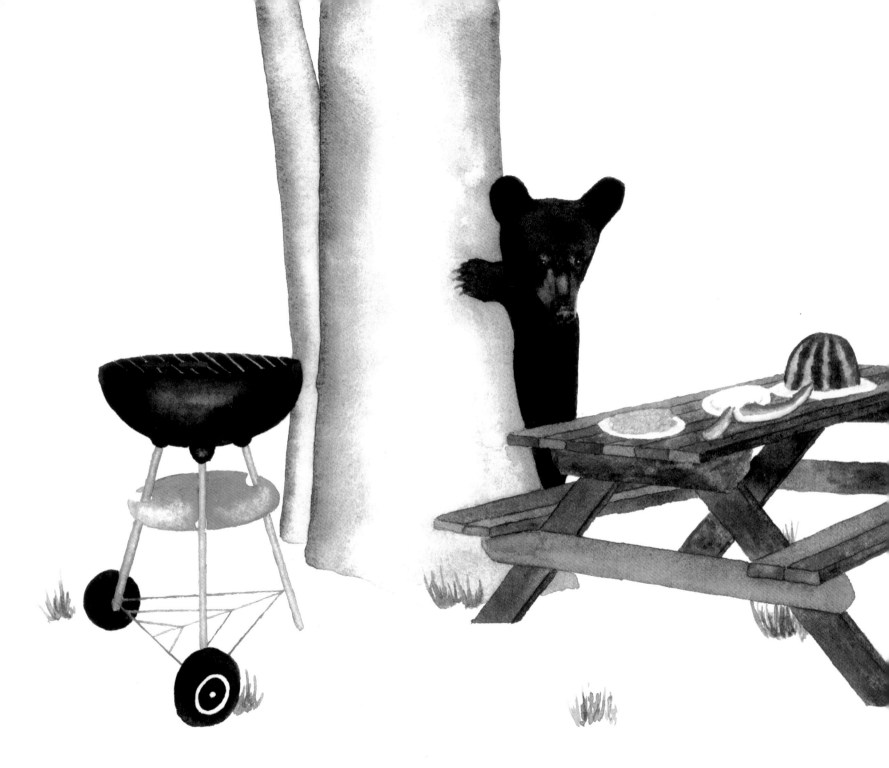

A curious bear will follow its nose
to find these yummy kibbles,
then quietly sneak on padded paws
and snatch a bite to nibble.

And once a bear tastes human food
that's rich in calories,
it finds new ways to grab some more
without a "thanks" or "please."

And claws that once were used on logs
are used to open sheds.
And teeth that once bit open fruits,
bite open cans instead.

And though at first it's funny
watching bears sneak past your lawn.
Broken sheds costs money, and then
people want bears gone.

So do your part to keep bears wild
by guarding food and trash.
Clean your grill, feed pets indoors,
and close the window sash.

For bears that don't eat human food
stay wild and safe and free.
How fun to be a little bear
up climbing in a tree!

the end